Write On!

COOL CHARACTERS

Written by
Charis Mather

KidHaven
PUBLISHING

Published in 2026 by
KidHaven Publishing, an Imprint of
Greenhaven Publishing, LLC
2544 Clinton St., Buffalo, NY 14224

Written by: Charis Mather
Edited by: Rebecca Phillips-Bartlett
Designed by: Jasmine Pointer

Cataloging-in-Publication Data
Names: Mather, Charis.
Title: Cool Characters / Charis Mather.
Description: Bufalo, New York : Kidhaven Publishing, 2026. | Series: Write On! | Includes glossary and index
Identifiers: ISBN 9781534550391 (pbk) | ISBN 9781534550407 (library bound) | ISBN 9781534550414 (ebook)
Subjects: LCSH: Authorship—Juvenile Literature | Creative writing—Juvenile Literature Classification: LCC PN159 M38 2026 | DDC 808.02-dc25

Manufactured in the United States of America

CPSIA compliance information: Batch #CSKH26
For further information contact Greenhaven Publishing LLC
at 1-844-317-7404.

Please visit our website,
www.greenhavenpublishing.com.
For a free color catalog of all our high-quality books, call toll free 1-844-317-7404
or fax 1-844-317-7405.

Find us on

Image Credits

All images are courtesy of Shutterstock.com, unless otherwise stated.

Cover – YummyBuum, Tutatamafilm, NotionPic, SpicyTruffel. Throughout – SpicyTruffel, NotionPic. 4–5 – Szasz-Fabian Jozsef, FAMILY STOCK. 6–7 – FamVeld, studiovin, Digital Storm. 8–9 – Jexy. 10–11 – Stanislav Danshyn, FAMILY STOCK. 12–13 – PeopleImages.com - Yuri A, Anton Vierietin, Casper1774 Studio, MOHSHINBD. 14–15 – ESB Professional. 16–17 – FOTOKITA, yalayama. 18–19 – ImageFlow, Suzanne Tucker. 20–21 – Prostock-studio, Yuriy Golub. 22–23 – KPG-Payless2, Sergey Novikov.

CONTENTS

Words that look like <u>this</u> can be found in the glossary on page 24.

YOU CAN WRITE

Who's your favorite character? A fearless adventurer? An evil genius? Maybe it is a character you created yourself. Character creation is one of the most fun parts of writing—at least, it is for me.

I am Professor Hoot. I love writing and teaching people how to write. With practice, anyone can write—including you! If you have never written your own characters before, you have lots to look forward to.

WHAT'S SO COOL ABOUT CHARACTERS?

If everyone in real life was exactly the same, life would be really boring. This is also true with made-up people. Good stories have characters with lots of different personalities and goals.

NOT EVERY CHARACTER HAS TO BE "COOL." ORDINARY CHARACTERS ARE OFTEN MORE RELATABLE.

<u>Realistic</u> characters can help readers connect to a story. Their struggles or mistakes can teach readers important lessons. Characters that are <u>larger than life</u> can make stories extra exciting.

DIFFERENT KINDS OF CHARACTERS

Protagonist

The protagonist is the character that the story follows. The protagonist's goals affect the direction of the story a lot. Protagonists are not always good or heroic, but readers are usually on their side.

Antagonist

Antagonists are characters who get in the way of the protagonist's goals. Antagonists are often seen as the villain, but they may not always be bad.

Side Characters

Side characters are often affected by the protagonists and antagonists. They might help the main characters or just exist in the background.

NIFTY NAMES

Usually, one of the first things that you find out about a character is their name. You want your readers to remember your characters, so you will need to give them names that are worth remembering.

Think about what kind of <u>impression</u> a name will make on a reader. If you want your readers to take a character seriously, give that character a sensible name. Otherwise, go wild!

Miss Majestic

Gabrielle the Glittering Girl

Little Lightning

Captain Flame

Sal the Superhero

Raya Sunshine

Power Kid

HOW DO YOUR CHARACTERS LOOK?

Not all stories come with pictures. Your job as a writer is to paint a picture with words. Well-written character descriptions help readers imagine exactly what characters look like. Try using exciting adjectives to describe your characters.

The way characters look can be important to the story. A character who looks frightening or mean might have trouble making friends. A character who looks kind might have lots of them.

CHARACTERS WITH FEATURES THAT STAND OUT ARE EASIER TO REMEMBER.

WHAT ARE YOUR CHARACTERS LIKE?

Deciding how your characters look is only part of character creation. You also need to work out what kind of personalities they have.

Questions to ask about your characters:

- What do they like and dislike?
- What do they want?
- Why do they act the way they do?
- What personality traits do they have?

REALISTIC CHARACTERS HAVE A MIX OF GOOD AND BAD TRAITS.

SHOWING, NOT TELLING

Sometimes, writers might tell you what a character is like.

However, characters are more interesting when the writer shows you what they are like.

I did not have to tell you the girl was scared—you could figure that out from how she acted!

A CHARACTER'S JOURNEY

Just like people in real life, characters make lots of choices. Lots of things can affect the choices that characters make, including their backstory, personality, goals, and feelings.

A backstory is everything that has happened in a character's past. Big life events, such as moving or getting injured, can affect how characters decide to act in different situations.

GROWING AND CHANGING

Think about the main characters in your favorite stories. Do they stay exactly the same throughout the whole story? Some characters change a lot, and other characters stay mostly the same.

Characters who change a lot are called dynamic characters. Characters who do not change much are called static characters. Before you start writing, think about how your characters could change by the end and why.

READ ON, WRITE ON

Isn't character creation cool? You can invent all kinds of characters using nothing but your imagination and some words. When you have decided what your characters are like, you could try drawing them.

IF YOU FIND WRITING HARD, DO NOT WORRY. EVERYONE GETS STUCK SOMETIMES!

One of the best ways to get better at making characters is to read other stories with interesting characters. The more you read, the more you will learn—so read on and write on!

GLOSSARY

adjectives	words that describe people, places, animals, or things
descriptions	statements that explain what something is like, such as how it looks or acts
features	parts of how someone looks
goals	things that people want and work toward
impression	the feeling that someone gets from something
larger than life	especially or unusually outgoing or dramatic
realistic	as seen in real life
relatable	easy to feel a connection with because of similarities
traits	qualities or characteristics of a person

INDEX

Write On!

TITLES IN THIS SERIES

COOL CHARACTERS

GREAT GRAMMAR

SUPER STORYTELLING

WONDERFUL WORDS

KidHaven PUBLISHING

ISBN: 9781534550391

9 781534 550391

Solar System Explorers

Venus

E.C. Andrews